Virtual Realms' Regulatory Revolution

Legal Challenges and Frameworks For Metaverse Governance

Kaylee Hemmings

Contents

1 Introduction to the Metaverse **5**
1.1 Defining the Metaverse 7
1.2 Technological Landscape 9

2 Legal Personhood in Virtual Worlds **13**
2.1 Digital Identity & Rights 15
2.2 Jurisdictional Challenges 17
2.3 Data Privacy Concerns 19

3 Intellectual Property Rights **23**
3.1 Ownership of Virtual Assets 25
3.2 Copyright & Trademark Issues 27
3.3 NFTs and Digital Scarcity 29
3.4 Licensing and Contracts 31
3.5 Enforcement Mechanisms 34

4 Contract Law in Virtual Environments **37**
4.1 Enforceability of Virtual Agreements 39
4.2 Dispute Resolution Mechanisms 41

5 Cybercrime and Security **45**
5.1 Virtual World Crime Prevention 47
5.2 Data Security and Breach Response 49
5.3 Combating Fraud and Scams 52

6 Consumer Protection in the Metaverse **55**
6.1 Misleading Advertising 57
6.2 Unfair Business Practices 59
6.3 Product Safety 61
6.4 Consumer Rights 63
6.5 Enforcement Agencies 65

7 Future of Metaverse Governance **67**
7.1 International Cooperation 69
7.2 Self-Regulation Initiatives 71

1 Introduction to the Metaverse

The metaverse isn't a single thing; it's more like a spectrum of interconnected virtual worlds, each with its unique features and functionalities. Imagine a persistent, shared, 3D environment where users interact with each other and digital objects using various technologies, blurring the lines between the physical and digital realms. This isn't science fiction; platforms like Decentraland and Sandbox are already demonstrating its potential, albeit in nascent forms. Understanding these early iterations is crucial for comprehending the overarching concept and the legal challenges it presents.

Central to the metaverse experience are immersive technologies like virtual reality (VR) and augmented reality (AR). VR creates entirely simulated environments, while AR overlays digital information onto the real world. These technologies, combined with advancements in 3D modeling, haptic feedback, and AI-powered avatars, deliver increasingly realistic and engaging user experiences, creating a compelling backdrop for commerce, social interaction, and even work. The level of immersion offered influences how we perceive and interact with virtual spaces, in turn creating unique legal implications that differ greatly from current online interactions.

Underlying many metaverse platforms is blockchain technology, enabling secure and transparent transactions and the creation of unique digital assets. Non-Fungible Tokens (NFTs) are a prime example, representing ownership of virtual items like land, artwork, or even virtual clothing. This digital scarcity, verified by the blockchain, creates a new economy within the metaverse, raising critical questions about ownership, intellectual property rights, and the enforceability of contracts concerning these virtual assets. The decentralized nature of many blockchain-based metaverses further complicates jurisdictional issues and presents a formidable challenge to traditional legal frameworks.

However, the very technological advancements that power the metaverse also introduce significant risks. Security breaches, data theft, and the potential for fraud are major concerns. Given the immersive nature of the experience, users are often more willing to share personal information within these environments, making them particularly vulnerable to malicious actors. Traditional cybersecurity measures need to adapt to the specific challenges posed by the metaverse, accounting for the integration of various technologies and the complexity of virtual interactions. Protecting user data and preventing cybercrime requires a multi-faceted approach, encompassing technical solutions, regulatory frameworks, and user education.

The increasing sophistication of the metaverse underscores the urgent need for a comprehensive legal framework. Current laws and regulations struggle to keep pace with its rapid evolution. Traditional jurisdictional boundaries become increasingly blurred in a virtual world accessible from anywhere with an internet connection. Enforcing contracts, resolving disputes, and protecting intellectual property in the metaverse require innovative solutions that account for its unique characteristics. This includes determining the legal status of virtual assets, clarifying liability for actions within virtual worlds, and addressing the complexities of cross-border transactions.

Consider the example of a virtual land dispute in a metaverse platform hosted overseas. Which country's laws apply? Who has jurisdiction to adjudicate the conflict? These questions highlight the crucial need for international cooperation and the development of consistent legal standards. The metaverse is not confined by geographical boundaries, and its legal governance must similarly transcend national jurisdictions. This requires an adaptive and collaborative approach, involving lawmakers, platform developers, and legal experts globally. Only through a concerted effort can we create a safe, secure, and legally sound environment that unlocks the full potential of this transformative technology. The future of the metaverse depends on it. Its success rests on the ability to establish a robust legal framework that balances innovation with protection.

1.1 Defining the Metaverse

The metaverse isn't a single, monolithic entity; rather, it's a spectrum of interconnected, immersive digital environments. Think of it less as a destination and more as a constantly evolving network of experiences—a shared virtual reality composed of persistent, interactive 3D worlds. This interconnectedness is a crucial aspect, fostering communication and interaction between users across different platforms and applications, blurring the lines between the physical and digital realms. It's a convergence of virtual and augmented realities, fueled by technological advancements in areas like blockchain, artificial reality (AR), virtual reality (VR), and sophisticated 3D modeling.

Defining the metaverse thus requires a nuanced approach, moving beyond simplistic descriptions. It's not merely about wearing a headset and interacting with a digital environment. The real power lies in the shared experience, the persistent nature of the virtual worlds, and the possibilities for interaction and creation that go far beyond the confines of traditional online interactions. This fundamentally alters our understanding of digital spaces, shifting from passive consumption of content to active participation in a dynamic ecosystem.

Several key characteristics help us grasp this complexity. Interoperability, meaning seamless movement between different platforms, is paramount. Imagine effortlessly transitioning from a virtual concert in one metaverse to a virtual art gallery in another, all while maintaining your digital identity and assets. This seamless transition is a core ideal, even if not entirely realized in practice. Immersion, achieved through VR/AR technologies, is another crucial component, creating a sense of presence and engagement that vastly exceeds traditional screen-based interactions. The depth of immersion can vary greatly depending on the technology used and the individual experience.

Furthermore, the metaverse's economic dimension is significant. Digital assets, virtual land, and in-world currencies are increasingly prominent, creating new economic opportunities and challenges. Decentralization, often facilitated through blockchain technology, represents another significant aspect, allowing for user-owned and user-governed virtual worlds. This decentralization contrasts sharply with the centralized control typical of many traditional online platforms, prompting crucial considerations for governance and regulation.

Understanding the metaverse requires avoiding simplistic generalizations. It is not a single, unified space controlled by one entity. Instead, it comprises a vast network of interconnected platforms and experiences, each with its unique characteristics and governance structure. This necessitates a flexible and adaptive approach to regulation, one that acknowledges the evolving nature of this digital landscape and its diverse participants. The legal and regulatory framework must evolve alongside the technological advancements, striving for a balance between innovation and the protection of user rights. This is not merely a technological challenge; it presents fundamental questions about identity, ownership, and responsibility within increasingly complex digital environments.

The implications extend beyond individual users. Businesses are exploring the metaverse as a new frontier for commerce, collaboration, and creativity. Governments, too, are grappling with the challenges of regulating this evolving space, grappling with issues of jurisdiction, taxation, and the enforcement of laws within virtual environments. The metaverse is not merely a technological innovation; it is a societal transformation, redefining our interactions, our economies, and even our understanding of reality itself. Its influence is profound and far-reaching, reshaping the way we live, work, and interact with the digital world. The need for clear, concise, and adaptable legislation is urgent, given the metaverse's rapidly evolving nature and its potential for both immense progress and significant harm.

The absence of a universally accepted definition, however, presents a significant hurdle. This lack of clarity creates ambiguity and complicates efforts to establish a robust regulatory framework. The ongoing development of metaverse technologies and applications further underscores the need for a flexible approach that can adapt to future innovations and challenges. It's not just about defining the metaverse; it's about understanding its dynamic and multifaceted nature and creating a governance system that can keep pace with its evolution. The task requires an interdisciplinary effort, involving technologists, legal experts, policymakers, and other stakeholders to ensure that the metaverse's potential benefits are realized while mitigating its risks. The ongoing dialogue and collaboration are crucial for shaping a future where the metaverse thrives as a safe, equitable, and innovative environment. This collective effort is vital in navigating the uncharted territories of this new digital frontier.

1.2 Technological Landscape

The metaverse isn't a singular entity; it's a tapestry woven from numerous technologies, each contributing uniquely to the overall experience. Virtual Reality (VR) and Augmented Reality (AR) are foundational, immersing users in digital environments or overlaying digital information onto the real world. These technologies, while distinct, are increasingly intertwined, blurring the lines between physical and virtual realities. Consider, for example, the implications of AR-mediated shopping experiences, where consumers can virtually "try on" clothes or furniture before purchasing. The legal ramifications of such interactions, from consumer protection to intellectual property rights, are considerable and require careful consideration.

Blockchain technology plays a crucial role, particularly concerning digital asset ownership and transactions. Its decentralized nature offers potential solutions for managing digital property rights and verifying authenticity, addressing concerns about fraud and counterfeiting. However, the inherent complexities of blockchain technology also introduce new legal challenges, such as clarifying ownership rights in decentralized virtual worlds and determining appropriate jurisdictional authorities for resolving disputes. This complex interplay of technology and law necessitates a multi-faceted approach to governance.

Beyond VR/AR and blockchain, other technologies like 3D modeling and animation tools shape the metaverse's visual landscape, influencing user interaction and experience. The intricacy of these environments requires robust legal frameworks that address potential issues, such as the protection of intellectual property embedded within the digital world. Think of the sophisticated digital artwork or unique virtual environments that can be created—protecting their creators' rights is essential for the continued innovation and growth of the metaverse.

Network infrastructure is equally crucial. High-bandwidth networks are required to support seamless interaction within the metaverse, and its reliability significantly impacts user experience and legal implications. Consider the liability of providers when network outages disrupt virtual events or transactions. This highlights the need for clear legal guidelines concerning service level agreements and potential compensation for users affected by network issues. The legal landscape must adapt to account for the unique challenges posed by this interconnected digital ecosystem.

The interaction between these technologies creates complex legal issues that demand innovative solutions. For instance, the intersection of VR/AR and blockchain technology in facilitating the sale and ownership of digital assets requires careful legal scrutiny. The lack of clear established norms increases the risk of disputes and legal uncertainty, hindering the overall development and adoption of the metaverse. A well-defined legal structure that acknowledges the novelty of this landscape is crucial. Understanding the technological foundation is the first step toward building a robust legal framework capable of addressing the myriad challenges and opportunities the metaverse presents.

The emergence of decentralized autonomous organizations (DAOs) also presents novel legal challenges. These self-governing entities, often operating within the metaverse, introduce complexities concerning accountability and liability. Determining how to hold DAOs accountable for actions within virtual worlds requires a nuanced understanding of both technological and legal frameworks. This necessitates exploring innovative solutions, perhaps through regulatory sandboxes, allowing for experimentation and the evolution of legal precedents in this evolving environment.

Finally, the rapid pace of technological development continues to outpace legal frameworks. The fluidity and innovative nature of metaverse technologies demand a flexible and adaptable regulatory approach. The need for international cooperation and collaboration on establishing guidelines is paramount to creating a consistent and reliable legal environment, enabling trust and fostering the metaverse's potential without sacrificing consumer protection or stifling innovation. The collaborative efforts of lawmakers, technologists, and legal experts are essential in navigating this unprecedented landscape and safeguarding the future of this rapidly evolving digital world.

2 Legal Personhood in Virtual Worlds

The metaverse, a seemingly boundless digital realm, presents a novel legal challenge: the question of legal personhood for virtual entities. Unlike physical entities with established legal standing, avatars and digital representations lack clear legal definitions. This necessitates a thorough examination of digital identity and the rights associated with it, rights that must be clearly defined and legally protected. This lack of clarity creates a significant hurdle for establishing consistent legal frameworks. For example, consider the implications of an avatar committing a virtual crime – is the user, the avatar's creator, or the platform itself responsible? The very nature of the metaverse, its decentralized and often borderless structure, makes assigning responsibility extraordinarily difficult.

Jurisdictional challenges are paramount. A virtual crime might occur in multiple jurisdictions simultaneously, confounding traditional legal processes. A user in one country might interact with a server in another, while the affected party resides elsewhere entirely. This lack of clear geographical boundaries complicates the enforcement of laws and creates loopholes that malicious actors can exploit. International cooperation becomes crucial in addressing this, requiring agreements between nations to establish cross-border legal mechanisms that specifically address the metaverse. This requires a fundamentally new approach to jurisprudence, acknowledging the unique challenges that transcend traditional national borders. The complexity increases exponentially as the metaverse's interconnectedness deepens, emphasizing the urgent need for international dialogue and regulatory harmonization. Without such cooperation, the metaverse risks becoming a haven for illegal activity.

Data privacy in virtual worlds demands a rigorous approach. Metaverse platforms collect vast amounts of user data, from behavioral patterns to personal preferences. This data is highly valuable, yet vulnerable to misuse or breaches. Existing data protection laws, designed for physical environments, may be inadequate to safeguard user privacy within the metaverse. Strengthening data protection regulations specifically for virtual environments is crucial. We need to consider enhanced data encryption, robust consent mechanisms, and rigorous accountability measures to prevent data exploitation. Furthermore, the potential for mass surveillance within the metaverse demands careful consideration and proactive legislative solutions to prevent abuse. Transparency and user control over their data must be paramount considerations in any future legal framework governing the metaverse. This necessitates a proactive approach, preventing privacy violations before they occur rather than simply reacting to breaches after the fact. A comprehensive framework must be built upon principles of user autonomy, data security, and accountability.

The absence of established legal frameworks for virtual entities poses significant risks. Without clear guidelines on ownership, liability, and responsibility, legal disputes are inevitable. The complexities extend beyond simple virtual property disputes. They encompass instances of virtual theft, harassment, and even virtual injury, which may result in real-world consequences. A robust legal infrastructure is needed, providing clear parameters and mechanisms for dispute resolution. This legal structure must accommodate the specific characteristics of virtual environments, ensuring fairness and efficiency in resolving conflicts. Innovative approaches, such as the creation of specialized virtual courts or the adaptation of existing dispute resolution mechanisms, should be explored to address this unique legal landscape effectively. The focus should be on creating a system that is both accessible and capable of handling the specific challenges posed by virtual environments.

2.1 Digital Identity & Rights

The metaverse, a sprawling digital landscape, presents unprecedented challenges to established legal frameworks. Central to these is the concept of digital identity and the rights it should afford. Unlike our physical identities, verified through birth certificates and other official documents, digital identities are often self-created, fluid, and exist across multiple platforms. This inherent flexibility, while offering liberating possibilities for self-expression and community building, simultaneously creates complexities for legal recognition and protection. Consider the implications of a virtual avatar experiencing harassment or theft; who is held accountable, and what legal recourse is available? This necessitates a comprehensive re-evaluation of existing legal paradigms.

Defining and safeguarding digital identities require a multi-faceted approach. Governments, tech companies, and users themselves must collaborate to establish clear guidelines and robust mechanisms for verification, authentication, and dispute resolution. Technological solutions, such as blockchain-based identity systems, can play a crucial role in enhancing the security and trustworthiness of digital identities. These systems, when coupled with appropriate legal frameworks, could offer verifiable proof of ownership and control, reducing ambiguity and fostering trust. However, the balance between security and privacy must be carefully considered; the benefits of secure identity systems shouldn't come at the cost of individual liberties.

The right to privacy in the metaverse is paramount. Data collected about users' virtual interactions, from browsing habits to in-world purchases, must be protected under rigorous data protection laws. Transparency in data collection practices and explicit user consent are vital. The anonymity often associated with digital identities doesn't negate the need for responsible data handling and protection against unauthorized access, misuse, or disclosure. Existing data protection regulations, such as GDPR and CCPA, need adaptation to the unique challenges posed by the metaverse; their principles, however, remain crucial in establishing a framework for responsible data governance. We must ensure that data protection laws are not merely an afterthought but are integral to the design and implementation of metaverse platforms.

Furthermore, the question of legal personhood for digital entities within the metaverse requires careful consideration. Should virtual avatars, capable of independent actions and interactions, be granted any form of legal recognition or rights? This is a significant philosophical and legal debate with far-reaching implications for the future of the metaverse. Such questions require thorough investigation, involving legal scholars, ethicists, and technologists to consider the implications of granting legal personhood to virtual beings. The complexity of these interactions requires thorough analysis, considering both potential benefits and risks carefully.

Jurisdictional challenges further complicate the issue of digital identity and rights. The metaverse transcends geographical boundaries, making it difficult to determine which legal system applies to disputes arising within it. Cross-border legal cooperation is crucial. International agreements and harmonized legal frameworks are necessary to create a consistent and predictable legal environment for users and businesses operating in the metaverse. The development of international standards and recognition of jurisdictional overlaps remains a complex but crucial step to establish a predictable legal environment within the metaverse. Without such collaboration, the metaverse runs the risk of becoming a lawless frontier, where users' rights are inadequately protected.

Ultimately, the protection of digital identities and rights within the metaverse is not solely a technical or legal challenge; it is a societal one. It requires a collective effort involving governments, businesses, and individual users to shape a future where the benefits of virtual worlds are accessible to all, while safeguarding individual rights and freedoms. This collaborative approach, embracing both technological innovation and legal reform, is essential for creating a secure, equitable, and thriving metaverse. The journey is far from over; proactive, collaborative efforts are critical to successfully navigate the challenges and unlock the transformative potential of digital identities in the metaverse.

2.2 Jurisdictional Challenges

Determining jurisdiction in the metaverse presents a unique and unprecedented challenge. Unlike the physical world, where geographical boundaries clearly define legal authority, the metaverse exists as a decentralized, interconnected digital space. This borderless nature makes it difficult to pinpoint which laws should apply to virtual events, transactions, or disputes. Imagine a virtual property dispute – where is the 'location' of the property for legal purposes? Is it where the server housing the virtual world is located? Or where the user accessing the property resides? The answers are far from clear, and this ambiguity significantly impacts the enforceability of laws and contracts.

The lack of clear jurisdictional boundaries creates significant legal uncertainty. Businesses operating in the metaverse face difficulties in complying with diverse and potentially conflicting regulations. For example, a company might be subject to data protection laws in multiple jurisdictions simultaneously, depending on where its users reside and where its servers are located. This not only increases compliance costs but also risks legal non-compliance, leading to potential penalties and reputational damage. Furthermore, it makes it incredibly challenging to establish a consistent regulatory framework, potentially hindering innovation and growth within the metaverse.

Individuals, too, face uncertainty. Their digital identities, assets, and activities may fall under the jurisdiction of several different legal systems, depending on the specific context. This lack of clarity makes it harder to protect their rights and interests, and it complicates dispute resolution. Imagine someone suffering financial harm from a scam within a metaverse platform. Determining which court has jurisdiction to hear their case might depend on the platform's location, the perpetrator's location, or even the victim's location – all of which can be geographically dispersed. This jurisdictional uncertainty directly impacts the efficacy of legal remedies, potentially leaving victims without recourse.

One potential approach is to establish international cooperation and agreements. Governments could collaborate to develop harmonized legal frameworks that address the unique challenges of the metaverse.

This may involve creating special metaverse-specific courts or tribunals with jurisdiction over disputes arising within virtual worlds. However, the sheer complexity of negotiating and implementing such global agreements should not be underestimated; differing national legal systems and political priorities could pose significant obstacles. Moreover, the speed of technological development in the metaverse may easily outpace the pace of international negotiations and legal harmonization.

Another approach might involve focusing on the principles of territoriality and user consent. This means that jurisdiction could be based on the location of the servers hosting the metaverse platform, and potentially on the users' acceptance of specific terms and conditions. However, relying solely on user consent can be problematic. Consumers might not fully understand the implications of such agreements, and there may be an imbalance of power between platform providers and users. The challenge lies in balancing the need for clarity and legal certainty with the need to protect user rights and prevent the exploitation of consumers.

Self-regulation by the metaverse industry could also play a role. Industry bodies could develop codes of conduct and best practices to address issues such as jurisdiction, data privacy, and dispute resolution. This approach can offer a more agile and responsive way to address emerging challenges. However, the effectiveness of self-regulation largely depends on the commitment and accountability of the industry players. Without strong enforcement mechanisms and transparent processes, self-regulation might not be sufficient to ensure the fairness and safety of the metaverse environment.

Ultimately, resolving jurisdictional challenges in the metaverse requires a multifaceted approach. A combination of international cooperation, domestic legislation, and self-regulation could provide a more robust and effective governance framework. Such a framework should strike a balance between facilitating innovation and protecting users' rights and interests. The development of clear legal standards and mechanisms for dispute resolution is crucial for fostering trust and confidence in the metaverse, paving the way for its responsible growth and adoption. The complexities involved demand a collaborative and iterative approach, involving governments, industry players, and legal experts working together to shape the future of legal governance in this rapidly evolving digital landscape. This necessitates ongoing dialogue, adaptation, and a willingness to embrace novel solutions to navigate the uncharted legal territories of the metaverse. The path forward will require ongoing engagement and a commitment to building a future where the rule of law is both effective and adaptable to the unique challenges of the virtual realm.

2.3 Data Privacy Concerns

Data within the metaverse is inherently different; its collection, processing, and use raise unique privacy challenges compared to traditional online environments. The persistent nature of avatars, the constant tracking of user behavior across multiple virtual spaces, and the integration of biometric data blur the lines between the physical and digital, creating a complex tapestry of privacy concerns demanding close examination. We aren't simply talking about website cookies here; we're discussing the potential for unprecedented surveillance and manipulation. The sheer volume of data generated within these immersive worlds necessitates a proactive, detailed approach to legal frameworks.

Consider the implications of virtual reality headsets capturing detailed biometric data – eye movements, heart rate, even facial expressions – all potentially linked to a user's persistent digital identity. This level of granularity surpasses what's typically collected by online platforms, magnifying the potential for misuse. This information could be used for targeted advertising, but also for more sinister purposes like profiling and discrimination, highlighting the need for robust safeguards. The very fabric of these immersive worlds demands a different perspective on data privacy, one that accounts for both the richness and the risks of the collected data.

Furthermore, the decentralized nature of many metaverse platforms complicates enforcement. Jurisdictional issues abound as users navigate across different virtual worlds and servers located in various countries. Establishing clear lines of responsibility for data protection becomes incredibly difficult. Who is liable when a data breach occurs?

How do we ensure consistent data protection standards across diverse platforms and jurisdictions? These questions need answers, and quickly, to ensure the metaverse remains a safe and ethical space.

The lack of clear legal definitions further complicates matters. Current data protection laws often struggle to keep pace with the rapid evolution of technology, let alone the emergence of entirely new digital ecosystems like the metaverse. Legislation designed for websites and mobile apps may not adequately address the unique challenges of persistent virtual worlds where data is collected and processed in far more nuanced ways. We need tailored legislation, not just repurposed laws. The current frameworks require substantial updates and often lack the clarity necessary to deal with the complexities of metaverse data.

Moreover, the concept of informed consent takes on a new dimension in the metaverse. Users may not always fully understand the extent of data collection occurring within a virtual world, especially if they are using multiple applications concurrently. The complexity of interactions and the immersive nature of the experience can mask the collection of granular data. This makes obtaining truly informed consent incredibly challenging, requiring a more transparent and user-friendly approach to data privacy notices and consent mechanisms. We must ensure users have the tools and knowledge to make informed decisions about the data they share.

To address these concerns, a multi-faceted approach is essential. Stronger data protection laws specifically tailored to the metaverse are necessary, ensuring clarity on data ownership, processing, and use. These laws must incorporate mechanisms for effective enforcement across jurisdictions and address the unique challenges of persistent virtual environments. International collaboration is key; a fragmented approach will only exacerbate the problem. Standardization of data privacy practices across different platforms is crucial, allowing for greater consistency and accountability.

Additionally, greater transparency is essential. Metaverse platforms must be more upfront about their data collection practices, employing clear and concise data privacy policies readily accessible to users. User-friendly interfaces that explain these policies in simple terms are crucial, ensuring that even less tech-savvy individuals understand the implications of their participation in the metaverse. We need to move away from dense legalese and toward clear, simple language that everyone can understand.

Ultimately, the successful navigation of data privacy concerns in the metaverse depends on a delicate balance between innovation and regulation. By fostering collaboration between policymakers, technologists, and users, we can create legal frameworks that protect user privacy without stifling the growth and potential of this transformative technology. The future of the metaverse hinges upon building trust, and that begins with establishing robust and transparent data protection measures. The task is complex, yet the need for action is undeniable. The metaverse has the potential to revolutionize various sectors; however, this potential must be pursued responsibly and ethically, placing data privacy at the forefront of the discussion.

3 Intellectual Property Rights

The metaverse, a digital realm teeming with creative expression and economic activity, presents unique challenges to traditional intellectual property (IP) frameworks. Unlike the physical world, the digital space offers unprecedented opportunities for replication and distribution, blurring the lines of ownership and potentially undermining established IP rights. Navigating this complex terrain requires a nuanced understanding of existing IP laws and their applicability within the virtual environment, along with a forward-looking perspective on adapting these laws to the metaverse's dynamic nature.

Consider the ownership of virtual assets. A digital avatar, a piece of virtual land, or a unique in-game item—these are all assets that users invest time, effort, and often money into acquiring. Yet, the legal basis for their ownership often remains unclear. While some platforms grant users limited rights to use these assets within their specific ecosystem, this doesn't necessarily translate to full ownership rights in the same way as a physical property deed. This ambiguity creates uncertainty for both creators and consumers, potentially hindering investment and innovation within the metaverse.

Copyright and trademark issues are further complicated by the ease of digital reproduction and distribution. The unauthorized copying and distribution of digital creations, from virtual clothing to architectural designs, pose a significant threat to creators' rights. Traditional enforcement mechanisms, often reliant on takedown notices and legal action, can be challenging to implement effectively in a decentralized and global space like the metaverse. The jurisdictional complexities alone can make it difficult to identify the appropriate authorities to enforce copyright or trademark infringements.

Non-Fungible Tokens (NFTs) have emerged as a potential tool to address issues of ownership and scarcity in the digital realm. By creating a unique digital certificate of authenticity linked to a virtual asset, NFTs offer a pathway towards establishing verifiable ownership. However, the legal implications of NFTs are still evolving. Questions remain regarding the scope of ownership rights granted by an NFT, the enforceability of these rights across different jurisdictions, and the legal protection offered to NFT holders against fraud or theft.

Licensing and contracting play a crucial role in defining the use and distribution of IP within the metaverse. Clear and well-defined licenses are essential to ensure the fair use of IP by users and to prevent unauthorized access or modifications. However, creating such agreements within a constantly evolving digital environment requires careful consideration of the specific context, including platform-specific rules and the evolving nature of virtual assets. Standardizing licensing practices and establishing robust contract enforcement mechanisms are necessary to encourage trust and facilitate transactions.

Enforcing IP rights in the metaverse demands innovative strategies. Traditional legal mechanisms alone might not be sufficient to address the scale and complexity of IP infringement in a decentralized space. Collaboration between platforms, rights holders, and lawmakers is crucial to develop effective enforcement mechanisms. These could include technologically-driven solutions such as blockchain-based tracking systems, automated copyright monitoring tools, and advanced digital watermarking techniques, alongside robust legal frameworks and international cooperation. Ultimately, a multi-faceted approach combining technological innovation with clear legal frameworks will be essential to safeguarding IP rights and fostering a thriving creative economy within the metaverse. The legal landscape is still developing, but these points provide a valuable foundation for navigating the challenges and opportunities.

3.1 Ownership of Virtual Assets

The ownership of virtual assets presents a unique and evolving legal challenge. Unlike tangible property, virtual assets exist solely in digital form, raising questions about their legal nature and the extent to which traditional property laws apply. Consider, for instance, a digital artwork purchased as an NFT. While the NFT serves as proof of ownership, its legal status remains contested; some jurisdictions might recognize it as a form of intellectual property, others as a collectible, and still others may not offer any clear legal framework. This ambiguity creates significant risks for both creators and consumers.

The decentralized nature of many virtual worlds further complicates the issue. Platforms like Decentraland or Sandbox operate on blockchain technology, where ownership is recorded on a distributed ledger. This eliminates a central authority to enforce property rights, making it more challenging to resolve disputes involving the theft or unauthorized use of virtual assets. A user might experience the loss of a valuable digital item within a game due to a platform's vulnerability or through malicious activity, and recovering this loss could be extremely difficult with few recourse options. The lack of a central, reliable mechanism of recourse could leave these users vulnerable.

This lack of clarity has significant implications for the metaverse economy. As virtual worlds become more sophisticated and integrated into our daily lives, the value of virtual assets is only going to increase. Digital real estate, in-game items, and virtual identities are becoming increasingly valuable commodities. The uncertainty surrounding their ownership can deter investment, hinder innovation, and potentially create instability in the digital economy. We need clear legal frameworks to define the ownership and transfer of virtual assets, to ensure trust and facilitate transactions within these digital spaces.

A practical approach might involve adapting existing intellectual property laws to the virtual context, recognizing that digital assets can encompass various forms of intellectual property, such as copyrights, trademarks, and patents. This will require careful consideration of the unique characteristics of virtual environments, such as their inherent mutability and the possibility of unauthorized copying or modification. The adaptation of existing frameworks should also incorporate the unique technological aspects, acknowledging the use of blockchain, smart contracts, and other technologies in determining ownership and transfer. Clear guidelines for registration, licensing, and enforcement would create a more secure and predictable environment.

Furthermore, the development of specific metaverse-focused legislation should not be discounted. Existing laws may need substantial modifications to be fully effective in dealing with the unique aspects of the virtual world. It might involve creating a specialized legal framework for virtual asset ownership, clarifying the legal status of various digital assets and specifying the responsibilities of both platform providers and users. This would require an international collaboration to prevent jurisdictional conflicts and ensure consistency in the application of laws across different metaverse platforms. International collaboration and standard-setting bodies could play a crucial role in this process, fostering the development of universally understood legal frameworks.

International harmonization is of paramount importance. As virtual worlds transcend geographical boundaries, inconsistencies in legal frameworks could undermine the integrity and stability of the metaverse economy. This is where international organizations and collaborations become essential in developing common legal standards, addressing cross-border disputes, and ensuring fairness and predictability in the metaverse legal landscape. The absence of such international collaborations could lead to significant challenges in enforcing legal rights and resolving disputes across jurisdictions.

Ultimately, the future of virtual asset ownership relies on a proactive and collaborative approach. Lawmakers, platform providers, and technology developers must work together to create a clear and consistent legal framework that protects the rights of both creators and users, while encouraging innovation and investment in the growing metaverse economy. Ignoring this urgent need for a legal framework may risk the future economic stability of virtual worlds and the potential benefits they hold. The development of this legal framework is not just about protecting intellectual property, but about ensuring the responsible and sustainable development of these emerging digital environments. It is about fostering trust and enabling a thriving virtual economy. Ignoring this vital aspect could hinder growth and innovation in this new technological frontier, thereby stalling the many societal benefits the metaverse promises.

3.2 Copyright & Trademark Issues

Protecting intellectual property in the metaverse presents unique challenges. Traditional copyright law, designed for physical works, must adapt to the digital realm's fluidity and accessibility. Consider, for instance, a virtual sculpture meticulously crafted and sold as an NFT: its copyright protection extends to its digital representation, but what about unauthorized 3D prints or in-world reproductions? The question of derivative works in a metaverse context necessitates careful legal analysis, encompassing not only the initial digital asset but also its various iterations and adaptations within the virtual environment. This complexity demands a nuanced understanding of copyright law's application to dynamic, user-generated content.

The metaverse significantly alters the landscape of trademark protection. Businesses establish virtual brand presence through avatars, logos, and virtual storefronts. Protecting these elements requires strategic trademark registration and enforcement. Infringement, however, is often more subtle in the metaverse; consider a competitor using a deceptively similar avatar or virtual storefront to mislead consumers. Establishing clear guidelines and legal precedents is essential to prevent trademark dilution and consumer confusion in this emerging space. This isn't a mere theoretical exercise; real-world examples show the potential for considerable losses from trademark infringement in virtual worlds. The need for proactive protection through robust trademark registration and monitoring is critical for brand survival in this new landscape.

NFTs, or non-fungible tokens, complicate the issue further. While often associated with digital art, NFTs can represent diverse virtual assets. The legal framework surrounding NFT ownership and copyright protection is still evolving. Determining who holds the copyright to an NFT—the

creator, the NFT owner, or perhaps both—is a complex question with significant implications for the marketplace. Moreover, the possibility of fractionalized NFT ownership adds another layer of intricacy, potentially leading to multiple copyright claimants. This evolving situation underscores the need for clear legal definitions and robust enforcement mechanisms to protect intellectual property rights in this novel context.
The enforcement of copyright and trademark rights in the metaverse presents significant challenges. Traditional legal mechanisms, designed for the physical world, are often inadequate. Jurisdictional issues, for example, become exponentially more complex in a decentralized, borderless virtual environment. The difficulty in identifying and tracking infringers adds another layer of complexity, especially given the often anonymous nature of online activity. Effective enforcement strategies require international cooperation and the development of novel tools and techniques to monitor and address infringement in a timely and efficient manner. The decentralized nature of many metaverse platforms further complicates matters, demanding creative legal solutions and innovative technological approaches. This issue requires international cooperation to ensure consistent enforcement and prevent the metaverse from becoming a haven for IP theft. This goes beyond simply adapting existing laws, it requires a fundamental re-evaluation of how we approach enforcement in a fundamentally different environment.
Developing effective strategies for protecting intellectual property in the metaverse requires a multi-pronged approach. This includes proactive trademark and copyright registration, robust monitoring of virtual environments for infringement, and the development of clear legal precedents to guide future disputes. Furthermore, fostering collaboration between legal professionals, technology developers, and metaverse platforms is crucial to create a robust legal framework that protects intellectual property rights while promoting innovation. International cooperation will be critical, enabling the development of harmonized legal standards and fostering effective cross-border enforcement. The long-term health of the metaverse depends on striking a balance between encouraging creativity and innovation and safeguarding intellectual property rights. Failing to do so risks stifling creativity and harming the meta-

verse's overall development. A proactive and collaborative approach is the only viable path forward. This is not just about adapting existing legal frameworks, but also about anticipating future challenges and establishing a legal infrastructure suitable for this evolving digital landscape. The stakes are high: the future of the metaverse itself rests on the ability to successfully address these issues. Failing to adequately protect intellectual property will ultimately hinder innovation and stifle the growth of the metaverse. It's an ongoing legal challenge that requires constant vigilance and adaptation.

3.3 NFTs and Digital Scarcity

The essence of NFTs lies in their capacity to create digital scarcity, a concept seemingly paradoxical in the infinitely replicable digital realm. Unlike physical assets, digital files are easily copied, rendering traditional notions of scarcity inapplicable. NFTs, however, leverage blockchain technology to create a verifiable, unique record of ownership for a digital asset, effectively transforming a readily duplicated file into a scarce commodity. This unique digital signature, permanently inscribed on the blockchain, confers a singular, provable ownership, thereby establishing scarcity where it previously didn't exist. This innovation presents intriguing legal challenges and opportunities.

Consider the implications for intellectual property. Traditional copyright law protects the expression of an idea, not the idea itself, leading to numerous copies of a work potentially existing. NFTs, however, introduce the possibility of associating unique ownership with each instance of a digital asset, even if the underlying file is easily duplicated. This raises complex questions about the interplay between copyright and the ownership rights conferred by an NFT. Does the ownership of an NFT grant exclusive rights exceeding those granted by copyright? This remains an area of ongoing legal debate, highlighting the need for clear legislative frameworks to address these emerging challenges.

The legal implications extend beyond copyright. Imagine a digital artwork sold as an NFT. The buyer acquires not just a copy of the artwork, but verifiable ownership of that specific instance, recorded on the blockchain. This ownership isn't merely aesthetic; it grants the buyer potential rights to control the further distribution or use of the artwork, depending on how these rights are defined in the smart contract attached to the NFT. These smart contracts, self-executing agreements encoded on the blockchain, add another layer of complexity to the legal landscape. Their enforcement and their potential conflicts with established legal principles present significant questions for lawmakers.

Furthermore, the decentralized nature of blockchain technology throws into sharp relief the challenges of jurisdiction. If an NFT is sold on a decentralized platform, where is the relevant jurisdiction for resolving disputes? Which legal system governs the terms of the smart contract? The answer is far from clear-cut, highlighting the transnational nature of these transactions and the urgent need for international cooperation to establish consistent legal frameworks. This jurisdictional ambiguity could deter investment and stifle innovation, unless international bodies work together to create harmonized legal guidelines.

The role of NFTs in the metaverse is even more significant, creating opportunities for new economic models and forms of ownership. Imagine virtual real estate, represented by NFTs, within a metaverse platform. The NFT wouldn't simply represent a digital image; it would signify provable ownership of a virtual plot of land, allowing the owner to develop it, lease it, or sell it. This virtual land could be as valuable, or more so, than physical land, particularly in expanding virtual economies. The ownership and use of this virtual land are entirely governed by the conditions specified within the NFT and its connected smart contract, setting a new precedent for property rights in the digital age.

However, this innovative use of NFTs presents significant risks. The potential for fraud and scams is substantial. The inherent complexities of blockchain technology and smart contracts can be exploited by unscrupulous actors, selling fake or worthless NFTs, or manipulating smart contracts to steal virtual assets or financial resources. The lack of a centralized authority makes it challenging to track and prosecute these actors, placing a greater emphasis on robust self-regulatory mechanisms within the NFT marketplace and strong legal frameworks able to traverse borders. Therefore, while NFTs offer immense potential for gen-

erating economic activity in the metaverse, careful legal and regulatory oversight is vital.
The creation of digital scarcity through NFTs is a powerful technological development with profound legal ramifications. Its impact on intellectual property, contract law, and jurisdiction requires careful consideration. The complexity of smart contracts and the decentralized nature of blockchain technology necessitates innovative legal approaches to ensure fair and effective regulation. International cooperation is critical in forging consistent legal frameworks that can adapt to the ever-evolving nature of the metaverse, striking a balance between innovation and protection. This nascent area of law demands proactive engagement from legal scholars, lawmakers, and industry stakeholders to navigate its intricate challenges and harness the significant potential of NFTs within virtual environments. The future of digital property rights depends on it. Ultimately, understanding the complexities of NFTs and digital scarcity is paramount for anyone seeking to understand the legal challenges and opportunities that define the metaverse. The lack of clarity currently poses a challenge, but simultaneously encourages innovation and adaptation. The path forward demands a thoughtful approach that balances progress with robust protection for all stakeholders.

3.4 Licensing and Contracts

Understanding the intricacies of licensing and contracts within the metaverse is crucial for both creators and users. Navigating this landscape requires a clear grasp of existing legal frameworks and their adaptability to this new digital frontier. Failure to do so can lead to significant financial and reputational losses. The unique characteristics of digital assets, coupled with the borderless nature of the metaverse, necessitate a nuanced approach to contract formation and enforcement. This chapter explores these challenges, offering practical guidance for secure transactions.
Effective licensing agreements are the cornerstone of protecting intellectual property in virtual worlds. These agreements must clearly define the scope of the license, specifying the permitted uses of the digi-

tal asset, the geographical limitations, and the duration of the license. Consider, for example, a creator licensing their virtual artwork for use in a metaverse game. The license should explicitly state whether the licensee can modify the artwork, incorporate it into other products, or sub-license it to third parties. Ambiguity in these areas can lead to costly disputes. Therefore, meticulous attention to detail is paramount. Such agreements must also account for updates and future versions of the licensed asset. This ensures that the licensing arrangement remains relevant and effective even as the metaverse evolves technologically. Furthermore, incorporating clauses relating to termination and dispute resolution will strengthen the agreement's overall robustness and protect the rights of both parties. Legal counsel specializing in intellectual property rights is highly advisable when drafting these crucial agreements. Careful consideration of these details can prevent potentially devastating conflicts.

Contracts within the metaverse often involve virtual assets, raising unique challenges concerning ownership and transfer. Blockchain technology plays a significant role, but its legal implications are still being developed. NFTs, for example, introduce verifiable ownership, yet enforcement of rights remains complex, especially across jurisdictions. The crucial consideration in crafting these contracts lies in clearly defining the ownership and transfer mechanisms for virtual assets. This demands precise language to specify the asset itself, methods of transfer, and the rights granted to the recipient. Smart contracts, often utilized within blockchain-based metaverses, add another layer of complexity, requiring an understanding of their legal enforceability. Moreover, the potential for cross-border transactions necessitates careful attention to differing legal systems and their respective interpretations of contract law. The increasing use of virtual currencies in metaverse transactions necessitates clarity regarding payment mechanisms, exchange rates, and potential risks associated with fluctuating cryptocurrency values. A well-structured contract will comprehensively address these aspects, anticipating and mitigating potential disputes.

The enforceability of metaverse contracts hinges on various factors, including the choice of governing law and jurisdiction. Because the metaverse transcends geographical boundaries, selecting a relevant jurisdiction can prove challenging, potentially leaving parties with little recourse should disputes arise. The legal precedent for virtual contracts is still evolving, which necessitates careful consideration of established contract law principles within the unique context of the virtual world. Jurisdictional clauses are therefore critical, explicitly stating which legal system will govern the contract and where disputes will be resolved. Additionally, careful consideration should be given to the enforceability of arbitration clauses within such contracts, as arbitration may offer a faster and more cost-effective mechanism for resolving conflicts compared to traditional court proceedings. This is especially important given the complex and often rapidly changing nature of the metaverse environment. Therefore, both parties need to carefully evaluate the potential advantages and disadvantages of utilizing arbitration for dispute resolution. Choosing the correct legal framework is pivotal in ensuring a robust, enforceable contract.

Beyond formal agreements, informal understandings and customary practices can also have legal implications within virtual environments. The decentralized nature of many metaverses might lead to the emergence of informal norms governing interactions, but these can be uncertain and potentially create complications. For instance, an agreement established through in-game chat could be subjected to interpretation based on general contract principles. These informal exchanges should ideally be recorded through reliable means, if possible, to serve as evidence of agreement. However, it is important to remember that relying solely on informal agreements is inherently risky. Moreover, these informal practices can evolve rapidly, potentially creating ambiguity and challenges for legal recourse. It is imperative for both users and creators to understand the potential legal ramifications of these implicit agreements within the evolving metaverse ecosystem. For greater clarity and certainty, it's advisable to reduce reliance on informal agreements and instead opt for more formally documented agreements whenever possible. This proactive approach can prevent significant future issues.

3.5 Enforcement Mechanisms

Effective enforcement of intellectual property rights (IPR) in the metaverse presents significant challenges. Unlike the physical world, the metaverse lacks clear geographical boundaries, making jurisdiction a complex issue. This jurisdictional ambiguity complicates enforcement actions, as determining which legal system applies to a particular infringement can be difficult, often requiring international cooperation which is currently underdeveloped in this space. This necessitates a proactive, multi-pronged approach, focusing on both legal and technological solutions.

One crucial element is the development of robust digital asset registries. These registries, potentially utilizing blockchain technology for enhanced transparency and immutability, could serve as reliable sources of proof of ownership for virtual assets. Establishing clear provenance and ownership records strengthens legal claims in case of infringement. This approach, while promising, requires careful consideration of data privacy concerns and the need for secure and accessible registry systems. Moreover, international standardization of such registries would greatly facilitate cross-border enforcement.

Furthermore, fostering collaboration between national and international IP enforcement agencies is paramount. Sharing information, coordinating investigations, and establishing mutual legal assistance treaties are essential steps towards creating a more effective global enforcement framework. This collaborative approach is crucial, considering the cross-border nature of many metaverse activities. Existing frameworks for international cooperation on cybercrime, for instance, provide a useful starting point and should be adapted to the specifics of metaverse IP infringement. The creation of a dedicated international body focused specifically on metaverse IP enforcement could be a potential long-term solution.

Technological solutions can also play a critical role. Advanced technologies like digital watermarking and blockchain-based provenance tracking offer innovative ways to protect and verify ownership of digital assets. These techniques can make it harder for infringers to operate undetected. Implementing such technologies needs careful consideration of their potential impact on user experience. They must not unduly burden creators or consumers.

Alongside these technical and international collaborative strategies, effective enforcement requires a clear legal framework. Laws need to be adaptable to the dynamic nature of the metaverse, and existing legislation needs to be interpreted and adapted to cover the unique aspects of virtual environments. This interpretation shouldn't be limited to adapting existing legal frameworks to a virtual setting, but should take into account specific nuances of virtual assets and the metaverse. The legal community must adapt swiftly and provide clear and understandable guidelines for businesses and individuals operating in the metaverse. This includes addressing the question of liability for platform providers hosting infringing content.

A crucial aspect is educating users about their IP rights and responsibilities in the metaverse. Public awareness campaigns can empower individuals to protect their creations and report infringements. This education must go beyond simply stating the laws, emphasizing practical steps to take when encountering infringement and available recourse. This must also extend to educational initiatives directed at creators, explaining best practices and risk mitigation techniques to protect their intellectual property. It is as important to teach creators about their rights as it is to teach users how to report infringements. The goal is a holistic understanding of the legal landscape.

Finally, developing effective dispute resolution mechanisms tailored to the metaverse is vital. Arbitration and mediation could provide faster and potentially less costly alternatives to traditional litigation, especially for low-value disputes. This is important because traditional litigation processes can be expensive, time-consuming, and geographically challenging in the context of the metaverse. Innovative online dispute resolution platforms, possibly integrated directly into metaverse platforms, could streamline the process and make it more accessible to users. The development of these platforms needs to consider principles of fairness, transparency, and accessibility. The key lies in efficient and user-friendly processes that promote timely resolution.

4 Contract Law in Virtual Environments

The burgeoning metaverse presents unique challenges to traditional contract law. Unlike physical contracts, virtual agreements often lack the tangible evidence and established legal precedents we're accustomed to. Consider a virtual land sale in Decentraland; the deed is a digital token, the transaction occurs on a blockchain, and the parties involved may reside in different jurisdictions. Establishing jurisdiction alone becomes a significant hurdle, requiring careful consideration of where the contract was formed, where the parties are located, and where the relevant assets are held. This lack of clear jurisdictional anchors can render enforcement difficult, potentially leaving parties without recourse in case of breach.

However, the absence of physicality doesn't necessarily equate to unenforceability. Many virtual agreements are perfectly valid and binding under existing contract law principles. A well-drafted contract, regardless of its digital format, can still adhere to the fundamental requirements of offer, acceptance, consideration, and intention to create legal relations. What's crucial is ensuring that the contract is clear, unambiguous, and explicitly addresses the specific digital nature of the transaction. This means outlining precisely what constitutes performance, how disputes will be resolved, and which laws will govern the contract, often necessitating careful choice of governing law clauses to address the transnational nature of many metaverse interactions. We must also remember that existing legal frameworks, such as the Uniform Commercial Code

(UCC) in the United States, may apply depending on the nature of the transaction, even if it unfolds in a virtual environment.

Dispute resolution presents a significant challenge within the metaverse, mirroring the jurisdictional ambiguities. Traditional litigation processes are often ill-equipped to handle virtual assets and cross-border disputes inherent in metaverse transactions. Arbitration offers a more agile and flexible approach. Arbitration clauses within metaverse contracts can significantly simplify dispute resolution by specifying a neutral forum and pre-defined procedures, avoiding the complexities and delays of traditional litigation across multiple jurisdictions. However, even arbitration requires careful selection of the arbitral institution and its ability to deal with digital evidence and virtual assets. Furthermore, ensuring that the award is enforceable in the relevant jurisdictions involved remains a key consideration, highlighting the complexities of global enforcement of such decisions.

Innovative solutions are emerging to streamline this. Smart contracts, self-executing agreements written in code, offer a level of automation that removes many ambiguities. These contracts automatically execute upon fulfillment of pre-defined conditions, reducing the likelihood of disputes. However, they're not a panacea. Smart contracts require rigorous coding and testing to avoid unforeseen consequences, and issues of interpretation and enforcement can still arise if the underlying code is flawed or if there's a dispute over the conditions of the agreement. They also remain susceptible to hacking and other security breaches, which can undermine their intended functionality. Moreover, their legal enforceability varies across jurisdictions, necessitating careful legal advice to ensure compliance.

Moreover, the development of specialized metaverse courts or dispute resolution mechanisms specifically designed to handle these unique challenges is becoming a growing area of focus for legal experts. These specialized entities will need to be well-equipped to deal with digital evidence, enforce judgments against virtual assets, and navigate the cross-border complexities of metaverse transactions. The establishment of clear and consistent legal guidelines is paramount. Harmonized international legal frameworks are crucial to build trust and predictability, stimulating economic activity within virtual environments. Such frameworks should address both the unique aspects of virtual contracts and incorporate existing international commercial law principles to establish a clear path toward fairness and efficiency within the metaverse. The lack of such uniformity currently poses a significant barrier to investment and growth in the metaverse economy.

Therefore, individuals and businesses entering the metaverse must prioritize legal counsel specialized in this emerging area. Negotiating and drafting comprehensive contracts that explicitly address the unique features of virtual environments is essential. Including clauses specifying jurisdiction, dispute resolution mechanisms, and the governing law is crucial to mitigate potential conflicts. Choosing appropriate dispute resolution methods like arbitration can significantly streamline conflict resolution. And finally, keeping abreast of the evolving legal landscape is essential to navigate the complex interplay of international and domestic laws governing the metaverse. The future of contract law in the metaverse will undoubtedly shape its economic and social development, requiring a proactive and adaptive approach from all stakeholders. Proactive engagement in the development of robust, clear, and globally harmonized legal frameworks is indispensable to ensure the metaverse's sustainable growth. Only through clear guidelines can we confidently navigate the potential, and the risks, of this new digital frontier. The continued development of virtual environments necessitates the development of tailored contractual frameworks, which will serve as a foundational element for stable development in the metaverse.

4.1 Enforceability of Virtual Agreements

The enforceability of virtual agreements presents a unique challenge, a fascinating intersection of established legal principles and cutting-edge technology. Consider a virtual land sale, conducted entirely within a metaverse platform, with a digital deed recorded on a blockchain. Is this transaction legally binding? The answer, unfortunately, isn't a simple yes or no. Existing contract law principles, rooted in physical interactions and tangible assets, are being strained by the virtual world's decentralized, borderless nature. Jurisdictional issues immediately arise; if the buyer resides in one country and the seller in another, which nation's laws govern the contract? The lack of a universally accepted legal framework for virtual worlds complicates matters significantly.

Determining the intention to create legally binding obligations is crucial. Unlike casual online interactions, virtual agreements necessitate clear and unambiguous terms, perhaps even utilizing digital signatures verified by reputable third-party providers. Simply clicking "I agree" within a virtual environment might not suffice; a more robust authentication process, reflecting the gravity of the transaction, is needed for enforceability. This isn't merely a technical issue; it demands a careful balance between ease of use and the rigor required for legitimate legal actions. The absence of such clarity could leave parties vulnerable to disputes with unclear avenues for resolution.

Furthermore, the inherent volatility of virtual assets adds a layer of complexity. The value of virtual land, for instance, can fluctuate dramatically based on in-game events, platform updates, or even broader market trends. Contractual clauses should explicitly address these risks, perhaps incorporating mechanisms for value adjustment or dispute resolution based on objective valuation methods. Failure to account for this inherent uncertainty could render even the most carefully crafted agreement vulnerable to challenges based on unforeseen changes in the virtual world's economy. Without a clear understanding of the risks involved, the whole process becomes increasingly opaque.

Enforcement presents another significant hurdle. Traditional legal remedies, like court orders or asset seizures, are difficult to apply within the metaverse's decentralized structure. Platforms themselves may offer internal dispute resolution systems, but their effectiveness varies widely, and their decisions often lack the same legal weight as a court judgment. This underscores the need for cooperation between legal systems and metaverse platforms, fostering frameworks for cross-border enforcement and harmonizing approaches to data retrieval and asset control within virtual worlds. A strong focus on collaborative efforts is, without doubt, the best route forward. This needs to be a collaborative and iterative process, and the resulting legal framework needs to be robust and adaptable.

The lack of established precedents further exacerbates the challenges. Legal systems are inherently reactive; they adapt to new circumstances, often lagging behind rapid technological developments. This creates a significant void where clear legal guidelines for virtual agreements are lacking. Consequently, innovative approaches are needed, perhaps involving the development of specialized metaverse courts or arbitration panels with expertise in both technology and law. These bodies would need to be recognized and respected by multiple jurisdictions to ensure effective enforcement of their decisions and to achieve some level of consistency across the different metaverse environments. Their expertise needs to span both technology and legal nuances, something that requires an immense amount of training and experience. This requires a holistic approach that fosters both legal and technological expertise in the newly emerging legal field.

Ultimately, ensuring the enforceability of virtual agreements requires a multifaceted approach. It necessitates clearer definitions of legal personhood within virtual worlds, robust authentication and verification processes for digital signatures and transactions, contract clauses that account for the inherent volatility of virtual assets, and effective cross-border enforcement mechanisms. It also demands collaboration between legal systems, metaverse platforms, and technology developers to create a stable, predictable, and just legal environment within the virtual realm. Without this collaborative and forward-thinking approach, the potential of the metaverse as a vibrant economic and social space will remain greatly hindered. The future of virtual commerce relies on addressing these challenges proactively and innovatively.

4.2 Dispute Resolution Mechanisms

Effective dispute resolution is crucial for the metaverse's sustainable growth. Without clear and accessible mechanisms, users will be hesitant to engage in transactions or participate fully, stifling innovation and hindering economic development. The current legal landscape, however, offers limited guidance, leaving a significant gap that needs immediate attention. Existing legal frameworks, primarily designed for physical interactions, often struggle to adapt to the unique characteristics of virtual environments.

The decentralized nature of many metaverse platforms further complicates matters. Jurisdictional issues arise when transactions involve users from different countries, each with its own legal system and enforcement capabilities. Determining which legal jurisdiction governs a particular dispute can be challenging and time-consuming, potentially discouraging resolution attempts. Furthermore, the absence of universally recognized digital identity systems makes it difficult to verify the identities of parties involved in a dispute, adding another layer of complexity. Imagine trying to resolve a contract dispute involving a user whose identity is only a string of numbers and not linked to any existing legal person, the process is cumbersome and potentially useless.

One approach to resolving these issues involves adapting existing dispute resolution methods. Arbitration, for example, offers a flexible and efficient alternative to traditional litigation, particularly suitable for cross-border disputes. Online dispute resolution (ODR) platforms, already used in various online contexts, could be adapted for the metaverse, providing a user-friendly and accessible platform for users to resolve disagreements. This would require developing standardized processes and procedures that are specifically tailored to the unique features of virtual worlds, potentially reducing some burdens. It's critical, however, to consider whether the existing arbitration frameworks are truly up to the complexities of metaverse transactions. A standard online arbitration might lack the expertise required to deal with the nuances of virtual assets or digital identities.

Mediation, another established method, offers a less formal approach focused on finding mutually agreeable solutions. Mediation's advantages lie in its potential for faster resolutions and lower costs compared to arbitration or litigation. In the metaverse context, mediation could be facilitated through virtual platforms, allowing parties to engage remotely from anywhere in the world. The success of mediation, however, depends on the willingness of the parties to cooperate, something that isn't always guaranteed, especially in scenarios involving high value transactions and strongly held positions. The level of trust required for such a method to work effectively might simply not be present in every case.

To effectively navigate these legal complexities, a multi-faceted approach is required. International cooperation is essential to create harmonized legal frameworks that address the jurisdictional challenges associated with cross-border disputes. Such agreements could involve establishing clear guidelines on jurisdiction, the recognition and enforcement of judgments and arbitration awards, and the development of common standards for digital identity verification. These frameworks should also acknowledge the need for specialized expertise, likely requiring international cooperation and investment in legal training, including the development of novel expert witnesses that can competently explain the intricacies of digital assets and virtual environments.

The development of industry-specific self-regulatory organizations (SROs) can also play a vital role. SROs can create codes of conduct, establish dispute resolution mechanisms, and provide guidance to participants in the metaverse. This approach could lead to faster, less costly resolution and could be particularly useful for disputes involving relatively low-value transactions. However, such SROs would need to be carefully designed to prevent capture by large corporations or individual interests, ensuring a fair and impartial system for all users, regardless of their size or influence. Without clear mandates and accountability mechanisms, the industry self-regulation may simply not work as intended. Careful consideration must be placed on the powers given and the degree of oversight required.

Ultimately, achieving effective dispute resolution in the metaverse requires a combination of legal frameworks, technological innovations, and self-regulatory initiatives. The goal should be to create a system that is both accessible and efficient, ensuring that users have confidence in the fairness and effectiveness of the dispute resolution process. This, in turn, will promote trust and encourage greater participation in the metaverse's economic and social activities. The future of the metaverse hinges on its ability to provide users with a fair and reliable system for resolving conflicts. Failing to address this fundamental need could significantly hamper its potential for growth and innovation.

5 Cybercrime and Security

The metaverse, with its immersive environments and interconnected networks, presents a fertile ground for cybercrime. Unlike traditional online spaces, the metaverse's complexity, coupled with the often-blurred lines between the physical and digital, demands a proactive and multifaceted approach to security. Understanding these unique vulnerabilities is the first step towards establishing effective preventative measures. We must move beyond simple analogies to the internet and recognize that the metaverse's interactive nature and realistic simulations introduce new vectors for attack.

Data security within the metaverse is paramount. The sheer volume of personal data collected, from biometric information to behavioral patterns, makes users highly vulnerable. Robust encryption, multi-factor authentication, and regular security audits are no longer optional; they are critical necessities. Furthermore, companies operating within the metaverse must implement stringent data protection policies, complying with existing regulations such as GDPR and CCPA while anticipating future legislation specific to virtual worlds. Failure to do so will not only expose users to significant risks, but also result in substantial legal and financial repercussions for the platforms themselves. The implementation of privacy-enhancing technologies, coupled with transparent data handling practices, will be key to building user trust and fostering a secure metaverse ecosystem.

Combating fraud and scams requires a different level of vigilance. The immersive nature of the metaverse can make users more susceptible to sophisticated phishing attacks, deceptive marketing schemes, and virtual asset theft. Education is key; users need to understand the risks involved in interacting with unknown entities or engaging in high-value transactions within the metaverse. Furthermore, platforms need to implement robust verification systems to identify and remove fraudulent actors, while also providing clear and accessible mechanisms for users to report suspicious activity. Real-time fraud detection systems, integrating artificial intelligence and machine learning, will prove invaluable in identifying and preventing fraudulent transactions. Active collaboration between law enforcement agencies, platform providers, and cybersecurity experts will be crucial in developing effective strategies for combating metaverse-related fraud.

Preventing virtual world crime involves a layered approach. This starts with strong passwords and multi-factor authentication for user accounts. Regular software updates and the use of reputable antivirus software are also crucial. However, it extends far beyond individual user responsibility. Platform providers must proactively implement robust security protocols, regularly auditing their systems for vulnerabilities and actively responding to threats. This requires investment in cutting-edge security technologies, as well as skilled cybersecurity professionals capable of managing the complex security challenges presented by the metaverse. Moreover, the establishment of clear legal frameworks and enforceable regulations is essential to deter criminal activity and facilitate the prosecution of offenders. International cooperation will be vital in addressing cross-border cybercrimes and ensuring the consistent application of laws across different jurisdictions.

Beyond technological solutions, addressing cybercrime in the metaverse requires a cultural shift. Promoting digital literacy and awareness among users is crucial in preventing many cybercrimes. Users should be educated on the various types of threats they may face, from phishing scams to malware attacks, and empowered with the knowledge and tools to protect themselves. This educational effort should extend beyond simple awareness campaigns to encompass interactive training and simulations that realistically demonstrate the risks and consequences of cybercrime. Similarly, platforms must prioritize user safety and transparency, proactively communicating security measures and providing accessible reporting channels for incidents. The collective responsibility of users, platforms, and law enforcement agencies will determine the security and safety of the metaverse. Ignoring this critical aspect jeopardizes not only individual users but the very future of this burgeoning digital landscape. We need a sustained effort to address cybersecurity risks and foster a culture of security from the ground up.

The metaverse is an evolving landscape, and the challenges of cybercrime and security are constantly changing. Staying ahead of the curve necessitates continuous monitoring of emerging threats, adaptation of security strategies, and proactive collaboration among all stakeholders. Only through a unified and adaptable approach can we truly ensure the safety and security of the metaverse, allowing its transformative potential to flourish without compromising the well-being of its users. The future of the metaverse hinges on our collective ability to anticipate, adapt, and ultimately overcome the ever-evolving threats of cybercrime. This requires a holistic strategy, integrating technological solutions with legal frameworks, user education, and consistent collaboration between all parties involved. This commitment to proactive security is not just about technological advancements; it's about building a responsible and trustworthy digital ecosystem.

5.1 Virtual World Crime Prevention

Prevention hinges on proactive measures, not reactive responses. A robust security framework, encompassing technological safeguards and user education, forms the bedrock of a secure metaverse. This necessitates a multi-layered approach, prioritizing prevention above all else. Implementing strong authentication protocols, like multi-factor authentication and biometric verification, significantly reduces unauthorized access. Regular software updates and vulnerability patching are paramount, constantly bolstering the system's resilience against evolving threats. The importance of user vigilance cannot be overstated; educating users on recognizing and avoiding phishing scams, malware, and social engineering tactics is crucial. This includes promoting secure password practices and fostering a culture of cybersecurity awareness.

The goal is to create a user base empowered to protect themselves from common online threats.

For law enforcement, a clear understanding of the virtual environment's intricacies is essential. This requires specialized training and tools to effectively investigate crimes within the metaverse. Developing investigative techniques tailored to the unique characteristics of virtual worlds is crucial, including forensic analysis of virtual evidence and effective collaboration with technology providers. Jurisdictional challenges present a significant obstacle; fostering international cooperation and harmonized legal frameworks is paramount to enabling cross-border investigations and the efficient prosecution of offenders. Building trust and transparency between law enforcement agencies and metaverse platforms is vital for seamless information sharing and coordinated efforts to combat crime.

Focusing on specific crime types clarifies the need for targeted preventative strategies. Virtual theft, a prevalent issue, requires robust asset protection measures, incorporating blockchain technology, smart contracts, and secure digital wallets. These techniques, however, require careful consideration to avoid unintended consequences, maintaining a balance between security and user autonomy. Addressing scams necessitates a collaborative approach involving platform providers, law enforcement, and consumer protection agencies. This collaboration should focus on proactive identification and removal of fraudulent activities, alongside public awareness campaigns to educate users on common scam tactics and methods of reporting them. These preventative actions must be underpinned by strong regulatory frameworks and swift enforcement mechanisms, creating a culture of accountability for malicious actors.

Furthermore, tackling harassment and online abuse demands a multipronged approach. Robust reporting mechanisms, clear community guidelines, and swift responses from platform moderators are essential. These measures must be combined with technological solutions, such as automated content moderation tools and AI-powered detection systems. However, such technology must be implemented judiciously to avoid unintended censorship or biases. A focus on fostering a positive and inclusive online community is crucial; providing users with tools to report abuse and mechanisms to seek support is necessary. Furthermore, the development of ethical AI solutions for content moderation and dispute resolution within virtual worlds remains a critical aspect of crime prevention. This includes the responsible application of artificial intelligence, ensuring transparency and accountability in the decision-making processes.

The prevention of virtual world crime is an ongoing process requiring continuous adaptation and collaboration. Technological advancements are constantly shifting the landscape, necessitating consistent updates to security protocols and preventative measures. Regular security audits and penetration testing are crucial for identifying vulnerabilities before they can be exploited. Moreover, close collaboration between metaverse platforms, policymakers, law enforcement, and cybersecurity experts is fundamental. Sharing best practices, conducting joint research, and fostering open communication are vital for developing effective and adaptable preventative strategies. The shared goal is to establish a virtual environment that is both innovative and secure, protecting users' rights and fostering a positive and safe online experience. The long-term success relies heavily on this commitment to a continuously evolving approach to safety. Ultimately, creating a safer metaverse requires a commitment from all stakeholders, a dedication to proactive measures, and an understanding that the fight against crime within these spaces is a continuous, evolving process. Ignoring this dynamic will result in a metaverse that is unsafe, ultimately undermining its potential for innovation and societal benefit.

5.2 Data Security and Breach Response

Robust data security is paramount in the metaverse, a realm where user interactions, transactions, and personal data are constantly exchanged. Failing to prioritize security invites significant risks, from financial losses to reputational damage and legal repercussions. Proactive measures are crucial, far outweighing the costs of reactive remediation. A multi-layered approach, incorporating both technical and procedural safe-

guards, is essential for creating a truly secure virtual environment.
Effective data security strategies must begin with a comprehensive risk assessment. This involves identifying potential vulnerabilities specific to the metaverse platform, including the types of data collected, the methods of data storage and transmission, and the potential points of access for malicious actors. Understanding these vulnerabilities allows for the targeted implementation of security controls, minimizing the risk of breaches. The process should be iterative, regularly reassessed to adapt to emerging threats and technological advancements within the metaverse. Ignoring this foundational step leaves the entire system vulnerable.

Beyond the risk assessment, robust encryption protocols are fundamental. Data both in transit and at rest must be protected using industry-standard encryption techniques, ensuring that even if intercepted, the data remains unreadable to unauthorized parties. This extends to all forms of data, including user credentials, transaction details, and personal information. Regular security audits, conducted by independent experts, should validate the effectiveness of these encryption measures and identify potential weaknesses before they can be exploited. Neglecting encryption is a serious oversight with potentially devastating consequences.

Beyond technical safeguards, effective data security requires robust access control mechanisms. These mechanisms, often involving multi-factor authentication and role-based access control, limit access to sensitive data to only authorized individuals and systems. Such restrictions should be rigorously enforced, with regular reviews to ensure adherence to established protocols and the timely revocation of access for employees who no longer require it. The meticulous implementation of access controls is an investment that protects against many internal and external threats.

Incident response planning is equally crucial. This involves developing a comprehensive plan that outlines the procedures to be followed in the event of a data breach. This plan should detail steps for containing the breach, mitigating its impact, notifying affected individuals, and cooperating with law enforcement agencies as needed. Regular training for staff on this plan is essential to ensure a rapid and effective response in a crisis, minimizing any negative effects. Failing to plan for the inevitable increases exposure and damages recovery efforts.

Data breach notification laws vary considerably across jurisdictions, emphasizing the importance of understanding the relevant legal obligations. Rapid and transparent communication with affected individuals and authorities is critical, mitigating potential legal liabilities and maintaining trust. Delaying notification can compound the negative impact of a breach, both legally and reputationally. Proactive compliance with all applicable legal frameworks demonstrates accountability and minimizes the ramifications.

The metaverse presents unique challenges in data security. The decentralized and borderless nature of many virtual worlds makes traditional approaches more difficult to implement. Cross-border data transfers require special consideration, along with the need for international cooperation to establish consistent legal standards and enforcement mechanisms. This complexity demands a proactive approach to identifying risks and developing strategies to address them effectively. Failure to do so exposes metaverse operations to a high degree of risk.

Legal compliance is a cornerstone of effective data security, especially given the growing body of data privacy regulations worldwide. Adherence to laws like GDPR, CCPA, and other relevant regional statutes is non-negotiable, encompassing not only data collection and use practices but also the security measures implemented to protect that data. Ignoring these legal frameworks exposes the organization to substantial fines and legal action, further impacting its reputation and operations. A dedicated legal team familiar with the evolving regulatory landscape is an invaluable asset.

Finally, fostering a culture of security awareness among all employees is paramount. Regular security training and awareness campaigns should educate staff on best practices, emphasizing the importance of strong passwords, recognizing phishing attempts, and reporting any suspicious activity promptly. This human element is often overlooked, yet it plays a pivotal role in preventing breaches and ensuring a robust security posture for the entire organization. A strong security culture empowers everyone to contribute to the overall security of the metaverse environment.

5.3 Combating Fraud and Scams

The metaverse, with its immersive environments and burgeoning economies, presents fertile ground for fraudsters and scammers. Unlike traditional online scams, metaverse fraud leverages the unique characteristics of virtual worlds, making detection and prevention more challenging. Sophisticated schemes exploit the trust inherent in virtual communities, targeting users with promises of quick riches or exclusive access to virtual assets. Understanding these tactics is crucial for developing effective countermeasures.

One prevalent form of metaverse fraud involves the manipulation of virtual assets. Scammers create counterfeit NFTs, promising high returns on investment, or they engage in pump-and-dump schemes, artificially inflating the value of a digital asset before selling their holdings at inflated prices, leaving unsuspecting investors with worthless items. These manipulations often hinge on exploiting the lack of clear regulatory oversight in many metaverse platforms, making it difficult to trace the perpetrators or recover lost funds. This requires a multi-faceted approach, encompassing user education, platform responsibility, and potentially, international legal frameworks that recognize and address the unique challenges presented by virtual assets.

Another significant area of concern is phishing scams, adapted for the metaverse environment. Scammers might create fake websites or in-world locations mimicking legitimate platforms to steal user login credentials, personal information, or cryptocurrency. These attacks can be incredibly convincing, capitalizing on the immersive nature of virtual worlds and leveraging social engineering techniques to gain users' trust. The use of deepfakes, realistic-looking AI-generated videos or images, further exacerbates this problem, making it difficult for users to distinguish between legitimate and fraudulent communications. Robust security protocols and user training on recognizing phishing attempts are essential components of mitigating this risk.

Beyond individual scams, organized crime groups are increasingly using the metaverse for more complex operations. Money laundering through virtual asset transactions is a growing concern, leveraging the relative anonymity offered by some platforms and cryptocurrencies. This necessitates the collaboration between law enforcement agencies, platform operators, and cryptocurrency exchanges to track and intercept illicit transactions, demanding improvements in transparency and tracking capabilities within the virtual economy.

Furthermore, the lack of clearly defined legal frameworks within the metaverse complicates enforcement efforts. Current legal systems often struggle to keep pace with the rapid innovation in virtual world technologies and business models. Jurisdictional ambiguity, arising from the decentralized and global nature of the metaverse, makes it challenging to prosecute offenders located outside a particular country's jurisdiction. This highlights the need for international cooperation in developing cross-border legal frameworks that address issues of cybercrime, fraud, and virtual asset theft. The creation of international agreements on data sharing and law enforcement cooperation is crucial.

Combating metaverse fraud requires a multi-pronged approach. Firstly, user education is paramount. Users need to be aware of common scams, understand the risks associated with virtual asset trading, and learn how to identify suspicious activities. Secondly, platform operators have a critical role to play in implementing robust security measures, including user authentication systems, fraud detection mechanisms, and secure transaction processing systems. Furthermore, collaboration between platforms, law enforcement agencies, and regulatory bodies is crucial for creating a secure and trustworthy environment. Finally, the development of clear legal frameworks, which address the unique challenges of the metaverse, is vital in providing a strong basis for prosecution and deterring fraudulent activities. Without a robust system of oversight and responsibility, the pervasive risks of fraud will cripple the expansion of the virtual realm's market. The future of the metaverse depends on our collective ability to overcome these significant security and legal challenges.

6 Consumer Protection in the Metaverse

The metaverse, a burgeoning digital realm, presents unique challenges to traditional consumer protection frameworks. Unlike the physical world, where geographical boundaries often dictate jurisdiction and enforcement, the metaverse's borderless nature complicates matters significantly. Consumers interacting within these virtual spaces are vulnerable to a range of issues demanding immediate attention and tailored solutions. This necessitates a comprehensive approach encompassing education, regulation, and robust enforcement mechanisms.

Misleading advertising is a primary concern. Companies can easily manipulate virtual environments, creating immersive experiences designed to deceive consumers into purchasing substandard or overpriced goods and services. The lack of clear physical presence adds to the complexity of verifying product claims, making it challenging for consumers to distinguish between legitimate businesses and fraudulent operators. Moreover, the anonymity afforded by many metaverse platforms can embolden unscrupulous actors to engage in deceptive practices with minimal fear of repercussions. This requires a multifaceted strategy; stronger regulatory oversight, including clear guidelines for virtual advertising, coupled with enhanced consumer awareness campaigns, is crucial for mitigating this risk. Independent verification services, specifically designed for the metaverse, could provide an additional layer of consumer protection.

Unfair business practices are rampant in the metaverse, mirroring those seen in the physical economy, yet often exacerbated by the virtual environment. Predatory pricing, hidden fees, and manipulative sales tactics are prevalent, targeting consumers who may be less familiar with the intricacies of metaverse transactions. The lack of tangible physical evidence makes it even harder for consumers to prove they've been subjected to unfair practices, making robust dispute resolution mechanisms essential. This necessitates a proactive approach from regulatory bodies, establishing clear parameters for acceptable business practices within virtual spaces. This would involve a concerted effort to translate existing consumer protection laws to the metaverse context, adapting them to the specific characteristics of virtual commerce.

Product safety within the metaverse is a less immediately obvious, but equally important, consideration. While we may not be concerned with physical injuries in the same way we are in the real world, virtual products can still cause harm. Malfunctioning virtual goods, buggy software causing data loss or financial harm, or experiences causing emotional distress are all legitimate concerns. The lack of consistent standards and testing procedures for virtual products makes consumers vulnerable to potentially harmful experiences. Here, a collaborative effort is needed between developers and regulatory authorities to develop standardized safety protocols and testing measures. This would ensure consumers are purchasing and using virtual products that meet minimum safety standards. Transparent labeling and clear warnings about potential risks would also prove vital.

Consumer rights in the metaverse must reflect the unique characteristics of this digital landscape. The right to redress, the right to information, and the right to choose, which are central to physical consumer protection, must be adapted and expanded for virtual environments. Ensuring these rights are protected requires a clear articulation of consumer rights within the metaverse, creating a legal framework that is both accessible and effective. This will not only empower consumers, enabling them to assert their rights, but also serve as a deterrent against businesses engaging in exploitative practices. This legal framework needs to be accompanied by accessible and user-friendly mechanisms for reporting issues and seeking redress.

Enforcement agencies play a crucial role in safeguarding consumer rights within the metaverse. Existing consumer protection agencies require adaptation and expansion of their jurisdictions to adequately oversee metaverse activities. International cooperation is paramount, given the metaverse's global reach and the jurisdictional ambiguities inherent in its borderless nature. Moreover, new, specialized agencies dedicated to metaverse consumer protection may be necessary to ensure effective enforcement. These agencies need to be well-resourced and equipped with the technical expertise needed to navigate the complexities of the virtual world. They must also be empowered to enforce regulations and impose effective penalties on businesses that violate consumer protection laws.

The creation of robust consumer protection in the metaverse is not merely a legal exercise; it is crucial for fostering consumer trust and ensuring the sustainable growth of this rapidly evolving digital realm. A comprehensive approach combining regulatory measures, consumer education, and effective enforcement is vital for creating a safe, fair, and trustworthy metaverse for all. The future of commerce and interaction within this space depends on it.

6.1 Misleading Advertising

Deceptive marketing practices in the metaverse present unique challenges. Unlike traditional advertising, where a physical product or service is readily observable, virtual goods and experiences often rely heavily on digital representations and user testimonials. This creates opportunities for manipulation, as the immersive nature of the metaverse can make it difficult for users to discern between genuine offerings and cleverly disguised scams. For instance, a virtual property might be advertised with images depicting luxurious amenities that simply don't exist within the game. The lack of physical presence and immediate tangibility makes verification far more difficult, potentially leading users to invest substantial sums in assets that hold little to no real-world value. Such practices underscore the urgent need for clear regulations and robust consumer protection measures.

The lack of consistent standards across different metaverse platforms exacerbates the problem. A company might employ misleading advertising techniques in one metaverse platform, escaping regulation or enforcement, only to repeat the tactic in a different one with little consequence. This jurisdictional ambiguity hinders effective oversight. Furthermore, the decentralized and often borderless nature of many metaverse platforms makes it challenging for authorities to pinpoint responsible parties and to enforce existing consumer protection laws. Investigations across jurisdictions are frequently time-consuming and expensive, especially when dealing with entities operating anonymously or through complex corporate structures. This highlights the critical need for international cooperation in regulating metaverse advertising.

The dynamic nature of the metaverse poses further complications. New platforms, virtual items, and marketing techniques emerge constantly, making it hard for regulators to keep up. Traditional advertising laws, designed for physical goods and services, often don't adequately address the subtleties of the virtual world. For example, the concept of "truth in advertising" requires nuanced interpretation when dealing with virtual assets whose value fluctuates based on in-game factors or community sentiment. Moreover, the use of virtual influencers and immersive advertisements adds another layer of complexity. Regulators must develop approaches that can adapt and evolve in response to these innovations.

Consumers require awareness and education. Many metaverse users are unfamiliar with the nuances of virtual transactions and advertising strategies. They may not be adept at detecting misleading claims or evaluating the credibility of virtual testimonials. A lack of media literacy in the digital space leaves them vulnerable to exploitation. Educational initiatives aimed at improving consumer awareness should be a key element of any regulatory framework. This can involve collaboration between government agencies, metaverse platforms, and consumer advocacy groups to create readily accessible educational resources, ensuring widespread understanding of potential risks and promoting informed decision-making.

Addressing this issue requires a multi-pronged approach. Firstly, robust legal frameworks are necessary, adapting existing consumer protection laws to the unique characteristics of the metaverse. These laws should clearly define misleading advertising in the virtual context, outlining specific prohibitions and penalties. Furthermore, they must specify who bears responsibility for enforcing these regulations – whether it's the platform operators, the advertisers themselves, or a designated government agency. Secondly, consistent international cooperation is vital to overcome the challenges posed by the metaverse's borderless nature. Developing harmonized standards and mutual recognition of enforcement actions will significantly improve regulatory efficiency. Thirdly, proactive collaboration between regulators, metaverse platforms, and consumer protection agencies is essential for continuous monitoring and rapid responses to emerging deceptive advertising practices. Only through such a cooperative, adaptable, and globally coordinated strategy can consumers be sufficiently protected in this evolving virtual realm.

6.2 Unfair Business Practices

Deceptive pricing tactics, a common issue in the physical world, readily transfer to the metaverse. Imagine purchasing virtual land advertised at a seemingly affordable price, only to discover hidden fees for utilities, maintenance, or even basic access features buried deep within lengthy terms of service. This lack of upfront transparency exploits consumers' unfamiliarity with the new marketplace. This is compounded by the pressure to purchase before a virtual land rush ends, leaving limited time to thoroughly review agreements. Regulations are needed to mandate clear, easily accessible pricing information and prevent this exploitation. Consumer protection laws should be adapted for the metaverse to mirror current standards for transparency in offline transactions.

The metaverse's immersive nature makes consumers particularly vulnerable to manipulative marketing techniques. Virtual advertisements subtly influence purchase decisions without their knowledge. For instance, product placements integrated seamlessly into virtual environments might subconsciously shape consumer preferences. This is ethically problematic and demands regulation to require clear disclosure of all promotional activities. Furthermore, deceptive endorsements, where virtual influencers promote products without disclosing their sponsorships, need robust oversight. These practices mimic existing problematic areas in online marketing, yet require adapted frameworks to address the unique presentation challenges of the virtual environment. It necessitates collaboration between lawmakers and technology companies to ensure transparency and consumer autonomy.

Many metaverse platforms operate with opaque algorithms that affect the user experience. These algorithms may prioritize certain vendors or products, creating an unfair advantage and effectively controlling the virtual marketplace. This can result in limited choice and artificially inflated prices. Users are often unaware of these underlying mechanisms shaping their purchasing decisions, highlighting a critical need for transparency and accountability. Regulators must mandate disclosure of these algorithms to allow consumers to make informed choices. The complexities involved require a balanced approach which addresses the innovation potential of the metaverse while protecting consumer interests. It is crucial to prevent a situation where a few powerful entities dictate the marketplace to the detriment of consumers.

Furthermore, the use of personalized data to target consumers with customized advertisements raises serious ethical concerns. Metaverse platforms collect extensive user data, tracking preferences, spending habits, and even emotional responses. This data is used to refine advertising strategies, potentially leading to manipulative targeting and exploiting consumer vulnerabilities. To ensure fair practices, strong data privacy regulations are essential. These regulations should grant users greater control over their data and prevent its misuse for manipulative marketing practices. This is not just about informing users what data is collected, but also enabling effective control of how this information is used. This requires a shift towards a consumer-centric data governance model, rather than relying solely on company self-regulation.

The sale of digital goods often lacks adequate consumer protection safeguards. Virtual items, from clothes to in-game assets, can be defective, easily duplicated, or even vanish without recourse. Unlike physical goods, digital assets lack tangible guarantees. This necessitates the creation of effective return policies, dispute resolution mechanisms, and clear standards for the quality and durability of virtual products. Furthermore, the lack of established standards for product safety poses considerable challenges. It is vital to develop safety standards, particularly for virtual reality interfaces, and enforce compliance to protect consumer safety. This interdisciplinary effort requires collaboration between consumer protection agencies, tech developers, and health organizations. Legal frameworks should anticipate these particularities, reflecting the inherent differences between physical and virtual marketplaces.

6.3 Product Safety

Ensuring product safety in the metaverse presents a unique challenge, demanding a novel approach to existing consumer protection frameworks. Unlike the physical world, where tangible products undergo rigorous testing and certification, virtual goods and services exist within a digital realm, demanding a new lens through which we assess safety. Consider a virtual rollercoaster; its design flaws might not cause physical harm, but could induce debilitating motion sickness or even trigger anxiety attacks in vulnerable users. The potential for psychological harm is a critical area requiring attention; regulatory bodies need to incorporate this into their safety assessments and standards.

This necessitates a shift in regulatory thinking. We cannot simply translate physical product safety regulations into the metaverse; a nuanced approach is required. The current legal frameworks often struggle to grapple with the intangible nature of virtual products. What constitutes a “defect” in a virtual item? How do we measure the “risk” associated with a virtual experience? Developing standardized metrics and methodologies for assessing virtual product safety is a priority. It requires collaboration between legal experts, technologists, and psychologists to establish acceptable levels of risk. This is where the new challenges reside, making this a particularly complex issue.

Moreover, the decentralized nature of the metaverse complicates enforcement. Many metaverse platforms operate internationally, making it difficult to establish clear jurisdiction and accountability. If a virtual product causes harm, which legal system should be responsible for redress? International cooperation and harmonization of regulations are essential to address this jurisdictional challenge. Without global cooperation, it is almost impossible for regulatory efforts to have the desired effect. The lack of a globalized framework significantly hampers effective regulation.

The responsibility for product safety should not solely rest on regulatory bodies. Developers and platform providers also bear a significant responsibility for ensuring the safety of their products and services. Clear guidelines and industry standards need to be established to guide developers in building safe and responsible virtual products. This could involve mandatory safety testing, the implementation of robust quality control processes, and clear labeling of products indicating their associated risks and suitability for different user groups. A collaborative effort between creators and regulators is a necessary measure to ensure the safety and reliability of virtual products.

Furthermore, user education and awareness are critical components of the product safety equation. Users need to understand the potential risks associated with using certain virtual products and services. This could involve clear warnings, safety instructions, and readily available information about potential risks and associated vulnerabilities. Empowering users with knowledge will aid them in making informed decisions. Users should be well-informed about possible side effects of virtual reality and augmented reality interactions.

Finally, dispute resolution mechanisms need to be readily available and easily accessible. Users who experience harm due to unsafe virtual products must have clear and efficient pathways to seek redress. This could involve establishing dedicated dispute resolution bodies specializing in metaverse-related issues or incorporating relevant dispute mechanisms in the terms of service of metaverse platforms. In this area, the focus must be on quick and fair dispute resolution, offering clear pathways for users to address product safety concerns. This is crucial for the future success of the metaverse as a safe and reliable environment.

6.4 Consumer Rights

Navigating the virtual marketplace requires awareness of your rights as a consumer. Unlike traditional shopping, where physical presence and established legal frameworks provide a degree of protection, the metaverse presents unique challenges. Understanding these challenges is paramount to ensuring a safe and fair user experience. Remember, your rights extend into the digital realm, though their application may require a nuanced approach. Companies operating within virtual worlds are still bound by existing consumer protection laws, adapted to the specific context of virtual transactions. This means false advertising, deceptive practices, and unsafe products remain illegal, regardless of the environment where the transaction takes place.

The lack of clear jurisdictional boundaries adds complexity. A virtual store might operate from a server in a different country than your location, creating ambiguity about which nation's consumer protection laws apply. This highlights the urgent need for international cooperation and harmonized legal frameworks to provide consistent consumer protection across metaverse platforms. Existing national consumer protection agencies have begun to address this issue, initiating investigations into misleading marketing practices and other violations within virtual spaces. It is, therefore, crucial to remain vigilant and report any suspected violations to the appropriate authorities.

One particularly vulnerable area is the purchase of virtual goods and services. Unlike physical products, the tangible value of a digital item can be easily manipulated. Deceptive pricing models, obscured terms and conditions, or the lack of clear refunds policies are prevalent issues. Scrutinize virtual marketplaces thoroughly. Before committing to a purchase, read reviews, compare prices across different platforms, and understand the terms and conditions of sale. Don't hesitate to ask questions or seek clarification if anything seems unclear or suspicious. Your right to accurate information and transparent transactions must always be upheld.

The nature of virtual transactions itself poses a challenge. Digital currencies, in-game assets, and NFTs raise unique issues pertaining to fraud and scams. Remember, the ease of anonymity online makes it imperative to exercise caution. Transactions involving unfamiliar parties or unknown digital currencies should be approached with extreme care. Verify the legitimacy of the seller and the platform before making a purchase, and only use secure payment methods. Many platforms now offer buyer protection programs, which provide recourse if a transaction goes wrong. Familiarize yourself with these programs and utilize them if necessary. Remember, your skepticism is your strongest ally in navigating the potential pitfalls of the virtual marketplace.

Furthermore, consider the possibility of product defects or failures in the virtual world. If you purchase a virtual item that proves faulty, or if a virtual service doesn't function as advertised, you are entitled to remedies. Your options may include requesting a refund, repair, or replacement, depending on the terms of sale and applicable legislation. Remember, while the format is digital, the consumer protection rights remain fundamentally the same. Documentation is crucial in establishing any claims. Save screenshots, transaction records, and any other evidence that demonstrates the issue and the nature of your attempts to obtain a remedy. This documentation will prove invaluable if you need to initiate a formal complaint or dispute.

While existing legal frameworks offer a foundation for consumer protection in the metaverse, their application is often complex and uncertain. However, the principle remains the same: Businesses cannot engage in misleading practices, sell faulty products, or violate consumer rights with impunity, simply because the transaction takes place in a virtual environment. Your rights as a consumer are not diminished by the shift to digital platforms; they are adapted and refined to address the specific challenges of these new marketplaces. The ongoing evolution of metaverse governance highlights the need for proactive engagement. Be informed, be vigilant, and be assertive in protecting your rights in this ever-evolving digital landscape. The future of consumer protection in the metaverse relies, in part, on the collective awareness and action of its users. By understanding your rights and actively demanding fair treatment, you contribute to building a safer and more ethical virtual marketplace for all.

6.5 Enforcement Agencies

The metaverse, a burgeoning digital landscape, necessitates robust consumer protection. Unlike traditional markets, the virtual realm presents unique challenges, demanding specialized enforcement. Existing agencies, however, often lack the expertise or jurisdictional reach to effectively address these challenges. This necessitates a multifaceted approach involving collaboration and adaptation of existing regulatory frameworks.

Consumer protection within the metaverse revolves around core principles mirroring those in the physical world: preventing fraud, ensuring product safety, and combating unfair business practices. However, the virtual nature of transactions and the decentralized architecture of many metaverse platforms introduce complexities. For example, establishing product safety for virtual goods requires novel definitions and enforcement methods, considering issues such as virtual item durability, functionality and potential impact on users' mental wellbeing. Digital assets, particularly NFTs, introduce further questions about ownership, authenticity, and consumer rights related to their purchase and use.

National consumer protection agencies will need to expand their purview. This expansion requires substantial investment in training and technological capability to monitor virtual marketplaces effectively and investigate complaints effectively. They'll need to adapt their investigative techniques to the digital environment, learning to navigate the technical complexities of blockchain technology, decentralized autonomous organizations (DAOs), and other metaverse-specific technologies.

International cooperation is critical. The metaverse transcends geographical boundaries, making jurisdictional issues paramount. A single nation's regulatory authority struggles to address cross-border transactions or scams originating from different jurisdictions. Therefore, fostering international collaborations amongst consumer protection agencies is vital for establishing consistent standards and effective enforcement across borders. This collaborative framework should involve sharing best practices, coordinating investigations, and establishing mutual legal assistance mechanisms to address cross-border consumer protection issues.

Self-regulatory organizations (SROs) within the metaverse itself hold significant potential. These organizations, comprised of platform operators, developers, and consumer representatives, could establish codes of conduct, dispute resolution mechanisms, and industry-specific standards for consumer protection. However, effective SROs require strong oversight from government agencies to ensure accountability and prevent conflicts of interest. They cannot replace government regulation but can act as a supplementary layer of enforcement, offering a more immediate and tailored response to certain consumer complaints.

Technological advancements will influence enforcement strategies. Blockchain technology's transparent nature can aid in tracking transactions and verifying the authenticity of digital goods. Artificial intelligence (AI) powered tools can assist in fraud detection and the identification of potentially harmful virtual goods or services. However, these technologies also present challenges. AI algorithms, for example, can perpetuate biases present in training data, potentially leading to unfair enforcement. Thorough consideration and mitigation of biases are crucial in integrating AI into enforcement processes.

Finally, empowering consumers themselves is a crucial aspect of consumer protection in the metaverse. Comprehensive consumer education initiatives are necessary to raise awareness about potential risks, safeguard their rights, and educate them about available recourse mechanisms. User-friendly reporting mechanisms and easily accessible dispute resolution services are paramount. Only through empowering consumers can they actively participate in shaping a secure and fair virtual environment. Such empowerment fosters a sense of responsibility, reducing the overall reliance on a reactive rather than proactive enforcement model.

7 Future of Metaverse Governance

International collaboration is paramount. No single nation can effectively regulate a space as borderless and interconnected as the metaverse. Shared legal principles, harmonized standards, and coordinated enforcement efforts are essential to address cross-border issues like data privacy violations, intellectual property theft, and virtual crime. This necessitates a global dialogue involving governments, international organizations, and industry stakeholders. The development of multilateral agreements, similar to those governing cyberspace, is crucial to creating a consistent and predictable legal environment within the metaverse. This is not simply a suggestion; it's a necessity driven by the interconnected nature of the technology itself and its rapidly growing global reach. The absence of a cohesive international framework would lead to regulatory fragmentation, creating legal uncertainties and hindering the metaverse's potential. Moreover, a fragmented approach is more vulnerable to exploitation by those seeking to evade regulations. Therefore, proactive collaboration is paramount to ensure the metaverse remains a safe, innovative, and economically viable environment for all.

Self-regulation is proving to be a critical component, complementing international cooperation. Industry-led initiatives, involving metaverse developers, platform operators, and content creators, play a significant role. These initiatives develop codes of conduct, best practices, and internal dispute resolution mechanisms. Examples include industry associations establishing ethical guidelines for virtual asset transactions or developing standards for data privacy. While self-regulation cannot replace government oversight, it can significantly contribute to efficient and responsive governance. The inherent dynamism of the metaverse necessitates flexible and adaptable governance structures. Self-regulatory efforts provide this flexibility, allowing for quicker responses to emerging challenges than traditional government legislation often allows. Furthermore, self-regulation can foster innovation by establishing clear guidelines that encourage responsible development and discourage harmful practices. However, the effectiveness of self-regulation hinges on its transparency, accountability, and enforcement mechanisms, something which needs to be carefully considered by all parties involved. Careful consideration of these factors is key to balancing the need for responsible growth with protecting user rights.

However, the balance between self-regulation and government oversight is delicate. While self-regulation offers agility and responsiveness, it risks being insufficient to address systemic issues or enforce robust protections for vulnerable users. Governments must therefore retain a crucial role in setting minimum standards, providing robust consumer protection, and enforcing legal obligations. This oversight is necessary to prevent the potential for market abuse or the exploitation of users. A collaborative approach, where governments and industry work together to define standards and mechanisms for enforcement, is the most effective strategy. This cooperative model allows industry to leverage its expertise and agility while ensuring government oversight protects the public interest. The development of sandbox environments, where new technologies and governance models can be tested and refined in a controlled setting, is another valuable approach. These test environments allow for experimentation and learning without compromising broader societal safety and legal frameworks. Such environments foster cooperation between industry innovators and regulatory bodies, laying the groundwork for more nuanced regulations.

The future of metaverse governance depends significantly on technological advancements. For example, decentralized autonomous organizations (DAOs) present an interesting concept for governance. DAOs utilize blockchain technology to establish transparent and decentralized decision-making processes within virtual communities. While promising, their effectiveness relies on robust code security, preventing vulnerabilities that could be exploited for malicious purposes. Moreover, legal recognition and enforcement mechanisms for DAOs must be further explored. Another evolving aspect is the use of artificial intelligence (AI) in governance. AI-powered systems could potentially enhance efficiency in areas such as dispute resolution and contract enforcement, while also contributing to more effective monitoring of virtual environments. However, the use of AI requires careful consideration of bias, transparency, and accountability to prevent the perpetuation of existing inequalities. It is crucial to consider the ethical implications and to develop robust safeguards against misuse. The metaverse's evolution will continue to present novel challenges requiring creative solutions and adaptable governance structures.

Ultimately, the most effective approach likely involves a multi-layered governance system. This includes international cooperation setting foundational principles, self-regulation mechanisms that provide flexibility and agility, and government oversight to ensure accountability and consumer protection. Technological developments will shape this future governance, requiring ongoing dialogue and collaboration between governments, industry, and users. The metaverse's success hinges on a collaborative, innovative, and adaptable approach to governance. This will not be a static process; instead, it demands constant monitoring, adaptation, and refinement as the technology evolves and its use cases expand globally. Only through this ongoing collaboration can we hope to create a robust, safe, and beneficial metaverse for all.

7.1 International Cooperation

Effective metaverse governance necessitates a global approach. The decentralized and borderless nature of virtual worlds renders national laws insufficient; a single nation's regulations cannot effectively address cross-border transactions, disputes, or criminal activities within a shared virtual space. Therefore, international cooperation is paramount to establishing a coherent and consistent legal framework. Without it, we risk a fragmented and potentially chaotic metaverse environment, hindering its potential benefits while exacerbating its inherent risks.

International collaboration offers several crucial advantages. Shared data collection and analysis would allow for a more comprehensive understanding of metaverse-related crime and illicit activities, facilitating more effective prevention and prosecution. Harmonized legal definitions of virtual assets, contracts, and digital identities would promote consistency and predictability for users and businesses alike, fostering trust and stimulating economic growth within the metaverse. Collaborative efforts could also streamline dispute resolution processes, offering users clear pathways to redress grievances regardless of their location or the jurisdiction of the relevant virtual platform. A unified approach is far more efficient than a series of conflicting national regulations.

However, achieving meaningful international cooperation presents significant challenges. Differing legal systems, cultural norms, and political priorities among nations can create significant obstacles. Finding common ground on complex legal issues, such as the recognition of virtual property rights or the enforcement of cross-border judgments, will demand considerable diplomatic effort and compromise. The lack of a single, overarching international body responsible for metaverse governance further complicates the task. Therefore, a multi-pronged approach may be most effective, involving the collaborative efforts of existing international organizations, intergovernmental agreements, and the development of model laws that individual nations can adapt to their specific contexts.

The development of model laws by organizations like the UN or specialized bodies within existing international legal frameworks could provide a valuable starting point. These models would ideally offer a standardized approach to key legal issues, such as virtual identity, data privacy, intellectual property, and contract enforcement within the metaverse. Simultaneously, establishing dedicated working groups or task forces composed of legal experts, technology professionals, and policymakers from various nations could facilitate the creation of effective mechanisms for collaboration and knowledge sharing. The ultimate goal is not to impose a rigid, global regulatory regime, but rather to develop a

flexible framework that respects national sovereignty while fostering the necessary consistency for a functioning metaverse economy.
Several promising examples of international cooperation in related fields offer valuable lessons. The development of international standards for data privacy, like the GDPR in Europe, demonstrates the potential for harmonizing regulations across jurisdictions. Likewise, international agreements on combating cybercrime, although still imperfect, underscore the importance of cross-border cooperation in addressing technology-related threats. In the context of the metaverse, successful international cooperation hinges on clear communication, mutual respect, and a shared understanding of the critical issues at stake. Building trust and fostering a collaborative environment between nations is crucial for achieving a coherent, secure, and thriving virtual world. The process will undoubtedly be lengthy and complex, demanding patience, flexibility, and a commitment to finding mutually beneficial solutions. However, the potential rewards – a safer, more stable, and more economically vibrant metaverse – far outweigh the challenges. The long-term implications of successful international cooperation in metaverse governance are transformative. It can unlock the metaverse's full economic potential, protect users' rights and safety, and ensure the sustainable growth of this rapidly evolving digital frontier.

7.2 Self-Regulation Initiatives

Self-regulation within the metaverse presents a compelling approach to governance, particularly in its nascent stages. This is crucial because the rapid evolution of metaverse technologies frequently outpaces the development of comprehensive legal frameworks. A bottom-up approach, where industry players proactively establish codes of conduct and best practices, can help bridge this gap, fostering a safer and more trustworthy virtual environment. Think of it like the early days of the internet, where industry self-regulation played a crucial role in establishing online etiquette and security protocols.
Successful self-regulation relies heavily on the active participation of key stakeholders. This includes metaverse platform developers, content cre-

ators, virtual world inhabitants, and even legal experts specializing in digital law. A collaborative environment is essential—one where diverse perspectives are heard and considered, leading to robust and inclusive guidelines. Without broad-based consensus, any self-regulatory framework risks being ineffective or even counterproductive, causing further fragmentation instead of unity. A successful initiative must address the diverse interests and concerns of all involved.

Several models for self-regulatory organizations exist, ranging from industry associations to independent regulatory bodies. Each has its advantages and disadvantages. Industry associations, for example, may lack the independence needed to hold their members accountable, potentially resulting in lenient enforcement. Independent bodies, on the other hand, might struggle to secure the necessary resources and cooperation from the industry. The optimal structure likely depends on the specific context, balancing the need for independence with the practical realities of implementation. Careful consideration of these nuances is critical for achieving effective self-regulation.

Establishing clear and enforceable standards is paramount. This necessitates detailed guidelines covering various aspects of metaverse operations, including data privacy, intellectual property protection, consumer protection, and dispute resolution. These standards should be transparent, accessible, and regularly updated to keep pace with technological advancements. For instance, clear guidelines on data collection and usage practices, mirroring existing regulations like GDPR, would foster user trust and minimize privacy breaches. Similarly, the development of standardized procedures for handling intellectual property disputes within virtual worlds would provide much-needed clarity and efficiency. Furthermore, effective mechanisms for monitoring compliance and enforcing standards are crucial. Self-regulatory bodies need to establish effective dispute resolution processes to address violations promptly and fairly. This could involve arbitration, mediation, or other forms of alternative dispute resolution, tailored to the unique characteristics of the metaverse. Regular audits and independent reviews can help ensure the integrity of the self-regulation framework and build public trust. Transparency in these processes is crucial, allowing external stakeholders to oversee the activities of the self-regulatory bodies.

A key challenge lies in achieving global harmonization of self-regulatory initiatives. The decentralized nature of the metaverse makes consistent enforcement across different jurisdictions extremely difficult. International cooperation and the development of internationally recognized standards are therefore critical. This might involve fostering dialogue and collaboration between self-regulatory organizations in various countries, potentially leading to the emergence of global best practices. The establishment of a multi-stakeholder forum, involving representatives from different jurisdictions and industry sectors, could provide a valuable platform for such collaborative efforts.

The success of self-regulation hinges significantly on its ability to adapt and evolve alongside the metaverse. Regular review and updates to the guidelines are essential to address new challenges and emerging technologies. Consider, for example, how the rise of new platforms and technologies could necessitate adjustments to existing standards concerning virtual asset ownership or data security. Continuous engagement with stakeholders ensures that the self-regulatory framework remains relevant and effective, thus maintaining its credibility and facilitating the responsible development of the metaverse. Ignoring this aspect would lead to an obsolete framework and potentially to the failure of self-regulation.

Ultimately, self-regulation in the metaverse requires a commitment from all stakeholders to create a responsible and trustworthy digital environment. It's a continuous process of collaboration, adaptation, and enforcement. While it may not be a panacea for all governance challenges, a well-structured self-regulatory framework can play a vital role in shaping the future of the metaverse, fostering innovation while safeguarding user rights and promoting a thriving virtual ecosystem. The proactive approach presented by these initiatives provides a much-needed layer of oversight, a safety net for users and developers navigating this uncharted digital territory. The collaborative and adaptive nature of such frameworks makes them uniquely suited to handle the dynamism of the metaverse, paving the way for a more responsible and equitable digital future. The involvement of legal experts specializing in technology law, international law, and intellectual property rights is essential in creating effective and sustainable self-regulation. This ensures that the guidelines align with existing legal frameworks and international standards, creating a solid foundation for growth within the metaverse environment.

www.ingramcontent.com/pod-product-compliance
Lightning Source LLC
LaVergne TN
LVHW022026200926
848481LV00007B/2554